£2-

THE WORLD OF MÁRQUEZ

THE WORLD OF MÁRQUEZ

A PHOTOGRAPHIC
EXPLORATION OF MACONDO

TEXT BY GABRIEL GARCÍA MÁRQUEZ
PHOTOGRAPHS BY HANNES WALLRAFEN

RYAN PUBLISHING
LONDON

First published in Great Britain by Ryan Publishing, an imprint of
Ryan Multimedia Ltd
11 Greek Street
London W1V 5LE.

The publisher gratefully acknowledges: Gabriel García Márquez
and Jonathan Cape for excerpts from *In Evil Hour, The Autumn of the
Patriarch, One Hundred Years of Solitude, Love in the Time of Cholera,
The General in his Labyrinth, Three Novellas* and *Collected Stories.*
Excerpts selected by Michael Diviney.
Photographer's acknowledgments appear on the final pages.

British Library Cataloguing in Publication Data.

Márquez, Gabriel García
World of Márquez: Photographic
Exploration of Macondo
I. Title II. Wallrafen, Hannes
III. Rabassa, Gregory
863

ISBN 1 870805 32 1

Printed in The Netherlands.

HANNES
IN MACONDO

GABRIEL GARCÍA MÁRQUEZ

I have always had great respect for readers who go off in search of the reality hidden behind my books. I have even greater respect for those who find it, because I've never been able to. In Aracataca, the Caribbean village where I was born, this seems to have become an everyday occupation. Over the last twenty years a whole generation of sharp children has grown up there, lying in wait for the myth-hunters at the railroad station so they can introduce them to the places, things, and even the characters from my novels: the tree that old José Arcadio was tied to, or the chestnut tree in whose shade Colonel Aureliano Buendía died, or the tomb in which Úrsula Iguarán was buried — alive, perhaps — in a shoebox.

These children haven't read my novels, of course, so their knowledge of the mythical Macondo can not have been acquired through them. The places, things and characters they show tourists are real only to the degree that the latter are willing to accept them as so. That is to say, behind the Macondo created by literary fiction there is another Macondo, even more imaginary and mythical, created by readers and authenticated by the children of Aracataca with a third visible and palpable Macondo which is, without a doubt, the falsest of them all. Fortunately, Macondo isn't a place, but a state of mind that allows people to see what they want to see and to see it as they see fit.

Last year, I experienced personally the high point of this poetical havoc while travelling along one of the icy rivers that descend from the Sierra Nevada range of Santa Marta and flow into Ciénaga Grande, the great swamp. It's a fact that the trip is made amidst dazzling waves of yellow butterflies and along a channel broken by frequent outcroppings of enormous polished white stones that are like prehistoric eggs, but the boatman assures tourists that when he was a child there were no stones that large nor were there any butterflies along the mountain streams, that they only appeared after *One Hundred Years of Solitude* came out.

In contrast, some years back in the village of Fundación there was an exhibition of furniture and domestic articles whose owner swore were from my grandparents' house in neighbouring Aracataca. The enterprise failed because nobody believed that these things were authentic. Yet, they really were the leftovers from an auction that had taken place after the death of my grandparents and which the purchaser had kept in storage until someone suggested that he set up the ill-fated museum in which nobody believed. The difficulty is in knowing who is closer to being right, those who believe in illusions or those who don't believe in the truth?

In the midst of so many superimposed Macondos there's another that rises up: that of the Dutch photographer Hannes Wallrafen, which could well be the most probable of all Macondos in this world because it's backed up by the conclusive documentation of some splendid photographs. I was strangely moved when in the soporific March heat of a ramshackle office in Cartegena de Indias, Hannes first showed them to me. I did not find any images equivalent to those which in some sense underpin my novels, and yet the poetic quality was the same. Later on, giving it more thought, I felt I had discovered that Hannes and I, each in his own way, had submitted the Caribbean coast of Colombia to the same set of poetic transpositions. It's not the direct reproduction of reality but the alchemy of fictional vision that, God willing, will end up someday being more real than reality itself. Manipulation? Of course, precisely what the alchemy of artistic creation has been and always will be. Because that's the way it has to be: the arts, like the prophecies of Nostradamus, can only be presented in codes and ciphers if they are to avoid self-defeat.

Hannes himself has told me of some experiences which mirror my own when I was getting my primary schooling as a writer by selling books on installment across the wilderness of the Guajira peninsula. Nobody could figure out who in a salt flat was going to buy a twenty-volume encyclopaedia or treatises on surgery, or how such an adventure could possibly be of any personal value to me. Still, it was those trips that in the end revealed to me the magic of a world without which my novels would have been impossible.

Hannes's experiences have been no less enigmatic or fruitful, although at first glance they may appear to be simple coincidences of everyday life. In his intensive exploration of the Caribbean he saw the dead crowned with roses, donkeys who performed miracles, statues of nobodies, people taking forever to die, wooden images of startled saints. He saw a man pushing a wheelbarrow that carried his own herniated scrotum. In the courtyard of the convent of Saint Peter Claver in Cartagena de Indias, he saw a woman sitting in a wicker rocking chair with two little girls dressed for their first communion dancing around her. In the market he saw a whole turtle being cooked alive in a pot of boiling water. As a child, I had witnessed the same sight, with one difference: the turtle had been cut up before being boiled and its heart was still beating in the pot. At lunch, in the midst of the already seasoned pieces, the heart continued beating. It was one of those extreme personal experiences that I never dared write about because I was afraid nobody would believe me.

Hannes insists, however, that he wasn't inspired by those apparitions of everyday life but, rather, by the secondhand ones that turn up in my books. Even though I still can't believe this, I can understand it. I pride myself on having a fine collection of great photographs and I can mention the numerous occasions when they have influenced my novels. The most memorable one for me was the photograph that suggested the tone I was missing to give the final touch to my novel about a Caribbean dictator. I'd already given up hope when, one blazing summer's afternoon in Rome, I saw a book of photographs on display in a bookstore on the Piazza di Spagna. It was placed in the window with the centre pages open and there was a photograph of an imperial palace somewhere in India, ravaged by the elements and devoured by the vegetation, on whose vines of yellow bellflowers monkeys were frolicking, as cattle wandered through the alabaster halls. At that moment *The Autumn of the Patriarch* was revealed to me in its entirety.

Trying to dig deeper in scrutiny of these mysteries is an attempt to invade the innumerable and slippery realms of creation, which only the most illuminated artists have the privilege of revealing without any explanations. And among them, clearly, there's an occasional photographer of human bondage like this wandering Dutchman who, while sailing along different currents, has arrived at the same port as I, with neither of us suspecting that we have both been the lucky victims of poetry's same tricks.

Translated by Gregory Rabassa

In January 1824, Commodore Johann Bernard Elbers, the father of river navigation, had registered the first steamboat to sail the Magdalena River, a primitive old forty-horsepower wreck named *Fidelity*. More than a century later, one seventh of July at six o'clock in the evening, Dr. Urbino Daza and his wife accompanied Fermina Daza as she boarded the boat that was to carry her on her first river voyage. It was the first vessel built in the local shipyards and had been christened *New Fidelity* in memory of its glorious ancestor. Fermina Daza could never believe that so significant a name for them both was indeed an historical coincidence and not another conceit born of Florentino Ariza's chronic romanticism.

We never heard that expression again until after the cyclone when he proclaimed a new amnesty for political prisoners and authorized the return of all exiles except men of letters, of course, them never, he said, they've got fever in their quills like thoroughbred roosters when they're moulting so that they're no good for anything except when they're good for something, he said, worse than politicians, worse than priests, just imagine, but let the others come back without distinction of color so that the rebuilding of the nation can be the task of all...

When his wife died he had set only one goal for himself: to turn his daughter into a great lady. The road was long and uncertain for a mule trader who did not know how to read or write and whose reputation as a horse thief was not so much proven as widespread in the province of San Juan de la Ciénaga. He lit a mule driver's cigar and lamented: 'The only thing worse than bad health is a bad name'.

*M*any displayed in their nudity traces of their past: scars of knife thrusts in the belly, starbursts of gunshot wounds, ridges of the razor cuts of love, Caesarean sections sewn up by butchers. Some of them had their young children with them during the day, those unfortunate fruits of youthful defiance or carelessness, and they took off their children's clothes as soon as they were brought in so they would not feel different in that paradise of nudity.

…and you, Juan Prieto, he said to me, how is your breed bull that he had treated himself with prayers against sickness so the worms would drop out of his ears, and you Matilde Peralta, let's see what you're going to give me for bringing back that runaway husband of yours in one piece, there he is, pulled along with a rope around his neck and warned by him in person that he'd rot in the stocks the next time he tried to desert his legitimate spouse, and with the same sense of immediate governance he had ordered a butcher to cut off the hands of a cheating treasurer in a public spectacle and he would pick the tomatoes in a private garden and eat them with the air of a connoisseur in the presence of his agronomists saying that what this soil needs is a good dose of male donkey shit…

She never got her reason back. When she went into the bedroom she found Petronila Iguarán there with the bothersome crinolines and the beaded jacket that she put on for formal visits, and she found Tranquilina María Miniata Alacoque Buendía, her grandmother, fanning herself with a peacock feather in her invalid's rocking chair, and her great-grandfather Aureliano Arcadio Buendía, with his imitation dolman of the viceregal guard, and Aureliano Iguarán, her father, who had invented a prayer to make the worms shrivel up and drop off cows, and her timid mother, and her cousin with the pig's tail, and José Arcadio Buendía, and her dead sons, all sitting in chairs lined up against the wall as if it were a wake and not a visit.

…and he was referring to no one but her, the godchild of the Duke of Alba, a lady of such lineage that she made the liver of presidents' wives quiver, a noble dame of fine blood like her, who had the right to sign eleven peninsular names and who was the only mortal creature in that town full of bastards who did not feel all confused at the sight of sixteen pieces of silverware, so that her adulterous husband could die of laughter afterward and say that so many knives and forks and spoons were not meant for a human being but for a centipede, and the only one who could tell with her eyes closed when the white wine was served and on what side and in which glass and when the red wine and on what side and in which glass…

He was the first man that Fermina Daza heard urinate. She heard him on their wedding night, while she lay prostrate with seasickness in the stateroom on the ship that was carrying them to France, and the sound of his stallion's stream seemed so potent, so replete with authority, that it increased her terror of the devastation to come. That memory often returned to her as the years weakened the stream, for she never could resign herself to his wetting the rim of the toilet bowl each time he used it.

…there was no other nation except the one that had been made by him in his own image and likeness where space was changed and time corrected by the designs of his absolute will…

They say he's the best in the district,' the colonel answered. 'He's worth about fifty pesos.' He was sure that this argument justified his determination to keep the rooster, a legacy from their son who was shot down nine months before at the cockfights for distributing clandestine literature. 'An expensive illusion,' she said. 'When the corn is gone we'll have to feed him on our own livers.'

Watching him putting in latches and repairing clocks, Fernanda wondered whether or not he too might be falling into the vice of building so that he could take apart like Colonel Aureliano Buendía and his little gold fishes, Amaranta and her shroud and her buttons, José Arcadio and the parchments, and Úrsula and her memories.

As soon as Pilar saw her come in she was aware of Meme's hidden motives. 'Sit down,' she told her. 'I don't need cards to tell the future of a Buendía.' Meme did not know and never would that the centenarian witch was her great-grandmother. Nor would she have believed it after the aggressive realism with which she revealed to her that the anxiety of falling in love could not find repose except in bed.

If inside time had the same rhythm as that outside, we would be in the bright sunlight now, in the middle of the street with the coffin. It would be later outside: it would be nighttime. It would be a heavy September night with a moon and women sitting in their courtyards chatting under the green light, and in the street, us, the renegades, in the full sunlight of this thirsty September.

It was the end. General Simón José Antonio de la Santísima Trinidad Bolívar y Palacios was leaving forever. He had wrested from Spanish domination an empire five times more vast than all of Europe, he had led twenty years of wars to keep it free and united, and he had governed it with a firm hand until the week before, but when it was time to leave he did not even take away with him the consolation that anyone believed in his departure.

From then on, he kept spare sets of teeth every-where, in various places throughout his house, in his desk drawer, and on each of the three company boats. Moreover, when he ate out he would carry an extra pair in a cough drop box that he kept in his pocket, because he had once broken a pair trying to eat pork cracklings at a picnic. Fearing that his nephew might be the victim of similar unpleasant surprises, Uncle Leo XII told Dr. Adonay to make him two sets right from the start: one of cheap materials for daily use at the office, and the other for Sundays and holidays, with a gold chip in the first molar that would impart a touch of realism.

A terrific job just occurred to me,' he said.

Ana realized that he'd been mulling over the idea since dusk.

'I'll go from town to town,' Damaso went on. 'I'll steal the billiard balls in one and I'll sell them in the next. Every town has a pool hall.'

'Until they shoot you.'

'Shoot, what kind of shoot?' he said. 'You only see that in the movies.'

…for at that time it did not look like a presidential palace but rather a marketplace where a person had to make his way through barefoot orderlies unloading vegetables and chicken cages from donkeys in the corridors, stepping over beggar women with famished godchildren who were sleeping in a huddle on the stairs awaiting the miracle of official charity, it was necessary to elude the flow of dirty water from the foul-mouthed concubines who were putting fresh flowers in the vases in the place of nocturnal flowers and swabbing the floor and singing songs of illusory loves to the rhythm of the dry branches that beat rugs on the balconies and all of it in the midst of the uproar of tenured civil servants who found hens laying eggs in desk drawers, and the traffic of whores and soldiers in the toilets, and a tumult of birds, and the fighting of street dogs in the midst of audiences because no one knew who was who or by whom in that palace with open doors in the grand disorder of which it was impossible to locate the government.

The carnival wagons arrived in the morning. Then came the trucks with the rented Indians who were carried into the towns in order to enlarge the crowds at public ceremonies. A short time before eleven o'clock, along with the music and rockets and jeeps of the retinue, the ministerial automobile, the color of strawberry soda, arrived.

From her cool personal surroundings the woman asked him if he wanted some lunch. He took the cover off the pot. A whole turtle was floating flippers up in the boiling water. For once he didn't shudder at the idea that the animal had been thrown alive into the pot, and that its heart would still be beating when they brought it quartered to the table.

When it was opened by the giant, the chest gave off a glacial exhalation. Inside there was only an enormous, transparent block with infinite internal needles in which the light of the sunset was broken up into colored stars. Disconcerted, knowing that the children were waiting for an immediate explanation, José Arcadio Buendía ventured a murmur:

'It's the largest diamond in the world.'

'No,' the gypsy countered. 'It's ice.'

The colonel didn't read the headlines. He made an effort to control his stomach. 'Ever since there's been censorship, the newspapers talk only about Europe,' he said. 'The best thing would be for the Europeans to come over here and for us to go to Europe. That way everybody would know what's happening in his own country.'

'To the Europeans, South America is a man with a mustache, a guitar, and a gun,' the doctor said, laughing over his newspaper. 'They don't understand the problem.'

*I*n the front he kept the main door and built two full-length windows with lathe-turned bars. He also kept the rear door, except a bit higher so that a horse could enter through it, and he kept a part of the old pier in use. That was always the door most used, not only because it was the natural entry to the mangers and the kitchen, but because it opened onto the street to the new docks without passing the square.

*R*esolved to dissipate even the dregs of the uneasiness that Patricio Aragonés had sown in his heart, he decided that those acts of torture would be the last of his regime, the crocodiles were killed, the torture chambers where it was possible to crumble every bone in the body one by one without killing were dismantled, he proclaimed a general amnesty, he looked to the future with the magical idea that came to him that the trouble with this country is that the people have too much time to think on their hands, and looking for a way to keep them busy he restored the March poetry festival and the annual contest for the election of a beauty queen, he built the largest baseball stadium in the Caribbean and imparted to our team the motto of victory or death...

THE AUTUMN OF THE PATRIARCH

everal hours must have passed since the massacre because the corpses had the same temperature as plaster in autumn and the same consistency of petrified foam that it had, and those who put them in the car had had time to pile them up in the same way in which they transported bunches of bananas. Trying to flee from the nightmare, José Arcadio Segundo dragged himself from one car to another in the direction in which the train was heading, and in the flashes of light that broke through the wooden slats as they went through sleeping towns he saw the man corpses, woman corpses, child corpses who would be thrown into the sea like rejected bananas.

Their wild and burdensome cargo was everywhere; the trunks full of clothing of people who had died before they'd been on earth, ancestors who couldn't have been found twenty fathoms under the earth; boxes full of kitchen utensils that hadn't been used for a long time and had belonged to my parents' most distant relatives (my father and mother were first cousins), and even a trunk filled with the images of the saints, which they used to reconstruct their family altar everywhere they stopped.

…and the light came out and it was no longer a March dawn but the noon of a radiant Wednesday, and he was able to give himself the pleasure of watching the disbelievers as with open mouths they contemplated the largest ocean liner in this world and the other aground in front of the church, whiter than anything, twenty times taller than the steeple and some ninety-seven times longer than the village, with its name engraved in iron letters, *Halálcsillag*, and the ancient and languid waters of the seas of death dripping down its sides.

*A*ll the birds of the air were in an uproar because of the kill, and the fishermen had to drive them away with their oars so they would not have to fight with them for the fruits of that prohibited miracle. The use of the mullein plant to put the fish to sleep had been prohibited by law since colonial times, but it continued to be a common practice among the fishermen of the Caribbean until it was replaced by dynamite.

She submitted in silence to the torture of the bed in the saltpeter pits, in the torpor of the lakeside towns, in the lunar craters of the talcum mines, while her grandmother sang the vision of the future to her as if she were reading cards.

On a morning like that, Dr Giraldo could under-stand the inner mechanism of suicide. It was drizzling noiselessly, the troupial was whistling in the house next door, and his wife was talking while he brushed his teeth.

'Sundays are strange,' she said, setting the table for breakfast. 'It's as if they were hung up quartered: they smell of raw animals.'

In order to be sure that she would not lose him in the shadows, she had assigned him a corner of the bedroom, the only one where he would be safe from the dead people who wandered through the house after sundown. 'If you do anything bad,' Úrsula would tell him, 'the saints will let me know.' The terror-filled nights of his childhood were reduced to that corner where he would remain motionless until it was time to go to bed, perspiring with fear on a stool under the watchful and glacial eyes of the tattletale saints.

Then, in a different tone, he added: 'As for now, I don't want to grow old at the head of any parish. I don't want to happen to me what happened to meek Antonio Isabel del Santísimo Sacramento del Altar Castañeda y Montero, who informed the bishop that a rain of dead birds was falling in his parish. The investigator sent by the bishop found him in the main square, playing cops and robbers with the children.'

The Dames expressed their perplexity.

'Who was he?'

'The curate who succeeded me in Macondo,' Father Ángel said. 'He was one hundred years old.'

Úrsula, for her part, thanked God for having awarded the family with a creature of exceptional purity, but at the same time she was disturbed by her beauty, for it seemed a contradictory virtue to her, a diabolical trap at the centre of her innocence. It was for that reason that she decided to keep her away from the world, to protect her from all earthly temptation, not knowing that Remedios the Beauty, even from the time when she was in her mother's womb, was safe from any contagion.

María Alejandrina Cervantes, about whom we used to say that she would only go to sleep once and that would be to die, was the most elegant and the most tender woman I have ever known, and the most serviceable in bed, but she was also the most strict. She'd been born and reared here, and here she lived, in a house with open doors with several rooms for rent and an enormous courtyard for dancing with lantern gourds bought in the Chinese bazaars of Paramaribo. It was she who did away with my generation's virginity. She taught us much more than we should have learned, but she taught us above all that there's no place in life sadder than an empty bed.

*M*acondo was already a fearful whirlwind of dust and rubble being spun about by the wrath of the biblical hurricane when Aureliano skipped eleven pages so as to not lose time with facts he knew only too well, and he began to decipher the instant that he was living, deciphering it as he lived it, prophesying himself in the act of deciphering the last page of the parchments, as if he were looking into a speaking mirror.

Then he saw the town on the other side of the track – the lights were on now – and it seemed to him that, by merely watching the train pass, it had taken him to another town. Perhaps from that came his habit of being present at the station every day, even after they shot the workers to death and the banana plantations were finished, and with them the hundred-and-forty-car trains, and there was left only that yellow, dusty train which neither brought anyone nor took anyone away.

There
are some
writers whose novels
are painstaking in their
attention to detail. Nothing is left
to the imagination. There are other writers
whose powers of evocation emanate from the
fact that they allow their readers to project their own
'photographic' image of the fictional reality described.
Gabriel García Márquez is such a writer.
Working on this project, I travelled to Colombia three times, in 1988, 1989
and 1991. It was at that moment when Gabriel García Márquez saw
my photos and exclaimed 'I want to do something with this',
that I decided to produce this collection. Just as Márquez
drew his inspiration from the people and places of
the Colombian Caribbean, my work was
inspired by his fiction and by the
scenes I found at Cartagena,
Aracatacta, Mompós,
Ciénaga and
Uribia.

*Without the
following people I
would not have been able
to make these pictures. Mieke
Vergeer, who persuaded me to
accompany her to Colombia in 1988. Mrs
Claudia de la Espriella and Mrs Sara Marcela Bozzi
of the Colombian Tourist Board. Gustavo Camacho and
Berenice Jiménez. Enrique, the owner of Hotel Bellavista. Carlos
Tatis, my guide in 1988 and his brother Gustavo Tatis, editor of El
Universal. León Ruíz, the photographer, who advised me in 1991. The
photographer Jean Paul Thomas and his wife Rosario Heins. Grupo Folclorico
Juventud de Barrio Chile. The painters Jean Pierre Acault and Cecilia Herrera. Antonio
Restom Bitar, my presidential candidate and the man in the dressing gown. Berto Jimeno who had a
great time watching rotting cowskulls. Vicky Ydios who lent me her wardrobe and Margarita Diaz
Petrocelli who posed in it. Teresa Roman de Zurec, Marcus Boranjo and Benedicta Cantilla Tafur. Virgillio de
Filippo, who showed me around Mompós. The students at the Arts academy: Elaine Montoya, Deborah Mateus,
Ana María Mercado, Ketty Figueroa, Hieber Quinteno, Elvis Cárdenas Velásquez and Alveiro
Trespalacios and their director Anibal Olier Bueno. Roberto Rios Jiménez and the members of his
Gustavo Castellon theatre group, Inez Martínez, Dafnis Osario, Alejandro Pérez and
Patricia Vega. The author Judith Porto de González and her pupils at the John F.
Kennedy School. The house of Sam Green and Casa del Marquéz de Valdehoyos.
But, also, I must not forget Mario Alvis Herrara, Moisis Alvarez Marín,
Pedro Blas Romero, Alberto Borga, Solvin Bowie, Ramiro
Cardona, Damian Elwes, Stefan Falke, Luis Herman
Giraldo, Armando Gonzáles Crismatt, Lucilita de
Ibelings, Daniel Lemaitre, Clara Mesa,
Paulina Padilla, Olga Lucia Paulhiac,
Alex Schutman, Eparquio Vega,
Zira de Vergara. And,
finally, Rally van
Heerdt.*

Hannes Wallrafen
June 1992